At the seaside

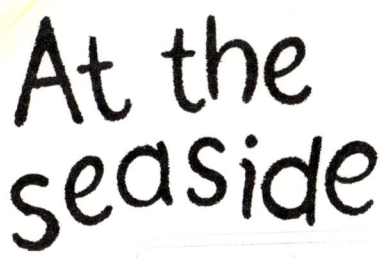

Written by Ruth Thomson
Illustrated by Charlotte Voake

PUBLISHED BY THE READER'S DIGEST ASSOCIATION LIMITED

The sky was blue.
The sun was hot.
Tim, Jenny, Mummy and Daddy decided to have a day out at the seaside.
"Don't forget your shrimp nets," said Mummy.

The beach was already very busy when they arrived.

Mummy and Daddy wanted to lie in the sun, but Tim and Jenny had other ideas.

First they built an enormous sandcastle.
Then they drew their names in giant letters on the sand.

They splashed and paddled
in the waves and played with a ball
along the water's edge.

They made a collection of shells
and seaweed and looked for
strange pieces of driftwood.

They built a high wall
and sheltered in the hole behind ...

until the tide came in
and washed the wall away.

After the picnic,
the children decided to go
exploring, with Daddy following
on and keeping them in sight.

"Let's explore the rockpools,"
said Tim, picking up their shrimp
nets. The rockpools were full
of the most amazing creatures –
shrimps and scuttling crabs,
sea anemones with waving tentacles
and rosy starfish.

"Let's look at that pool," said Jenny pointing towards one near a big rock.

As they got near, they could hear
a most curious noise
coming from behind the rock.

Whatever could it be?

Tim and Jenny peeped around the rock, just far enough to spy an enormous pair of black boots with silver buckles on them.

They peeped a bit further ...

... and then they saw a dirty pair
of patched trousers held up by a strong
leather belt. Tucked into the belt
was a gleaming, sharp knife.
Tim and Jenny were open-mouthed.

They peeped a bit further ...

. . . and then they saw
two hairy, folded arms.
A telescope was clutched in
one hand – a clay pipe was
clutched in the other.
Who could this be?

Feeling very brave,
Tim and Jenny peeped
right round the rock.

There, lying fast asleep
and snoring extremely loudly
was the fiercest person
they had ever seen.

"It's a real, live pirate,"
hissed Jenny.
"Don't be funny," said Tim.
"There aren't any pirates
any more."
"I'm going to ask him," said Jenny
feeling very bold.

"Excuse me," she said very loudly.
The man opened one eye.

"Excuse me," said Jenny again,
"but are you a real pirate?"
He opened the other eye.
"Scuttle that schooner,"
he roared. "Of course I am!"
He stood up, puffed himself
to his full height and scowled.

"But whatever are you doing
on this beach?" asked Tim.
"I'm shipwrecked, that's what,"
replied the pirate crossly.
"I've lost my ship,
I've lost my crew
and, worst of all,
I've lost my treasure."

Tim and Jenny felt rather sorry
for the pirate. Just then
Daddy came forward and they
all decided to help the pirate.

"I know where you might find some treasure. Follow us," said Daddy.
Off they went along the beach, past the Punch and Judy show.

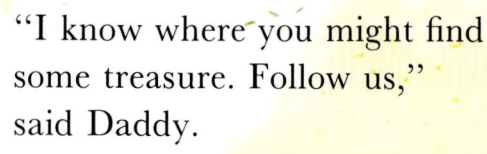

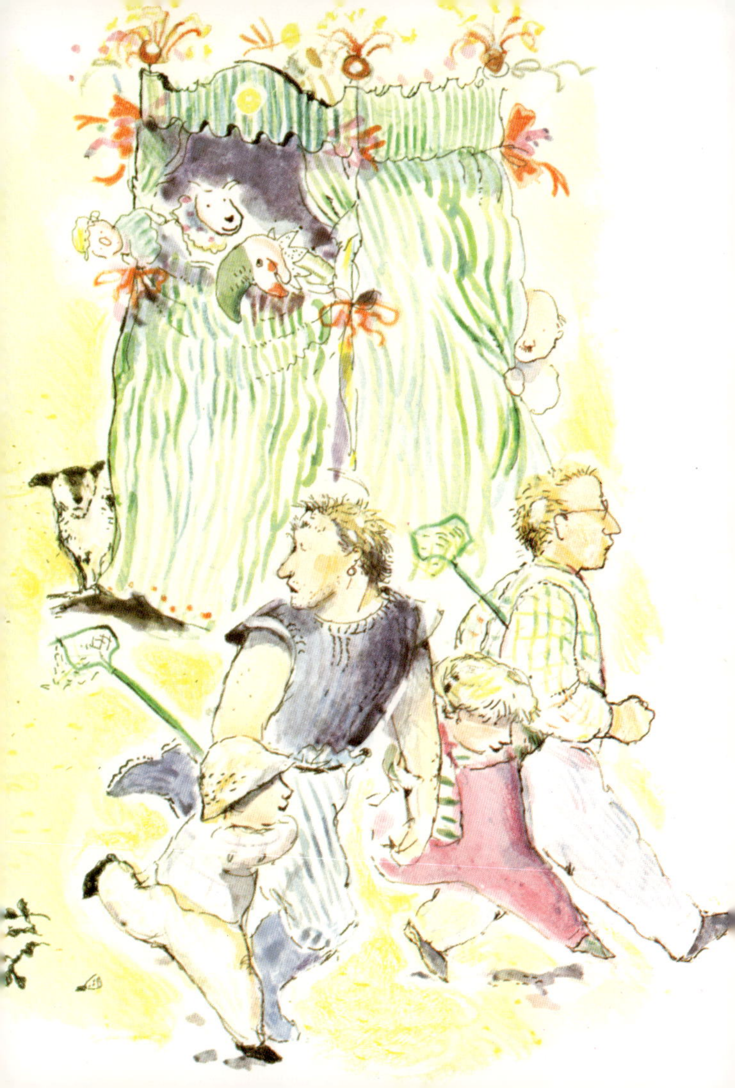

They went past the donkey rides
and the ice-cream man.
Everybody turned to stare.

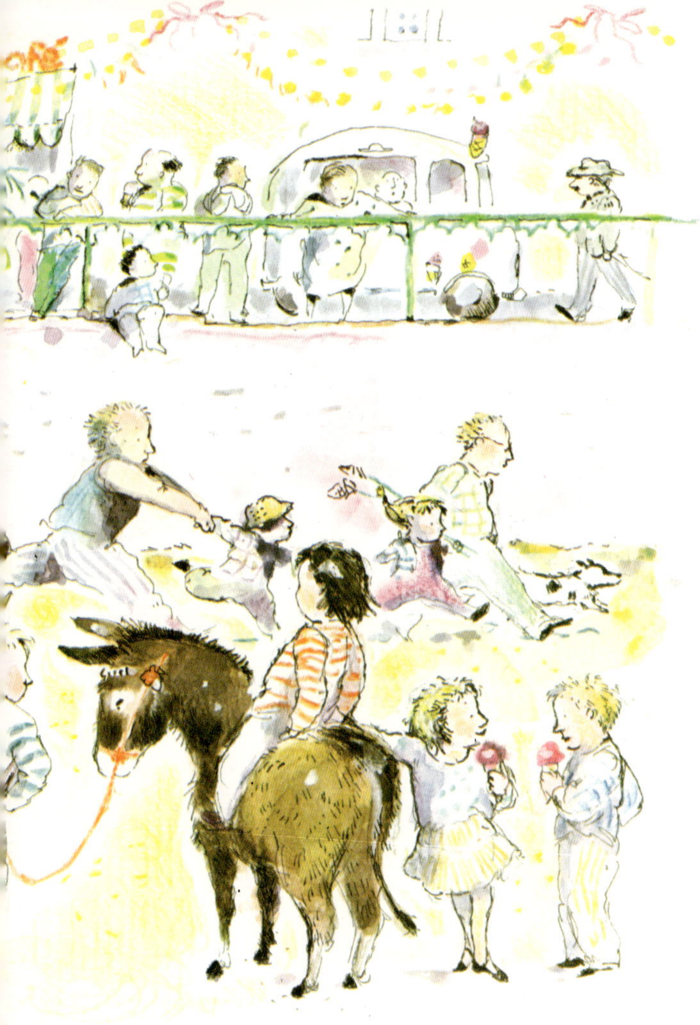

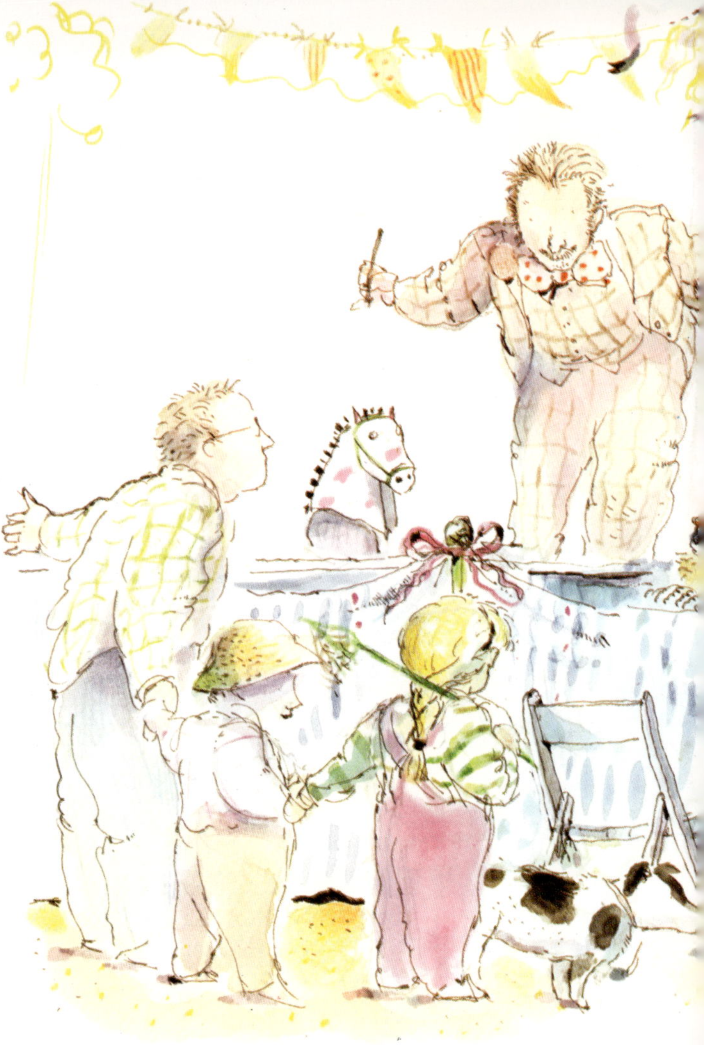

Daddy stopped at the stage.
"Hurry up, hurry up," said a
man in a check suit and a funny tie.
"We're about to begin."
There was a loud roll of drums
and the band began to play.

One by one, a strange assortment of people came to the stage.

There was a clumsy clown, a frilly fairy and a spotted horse.

There was a wizened wizard,
a very grand lady
and a rather big baby.

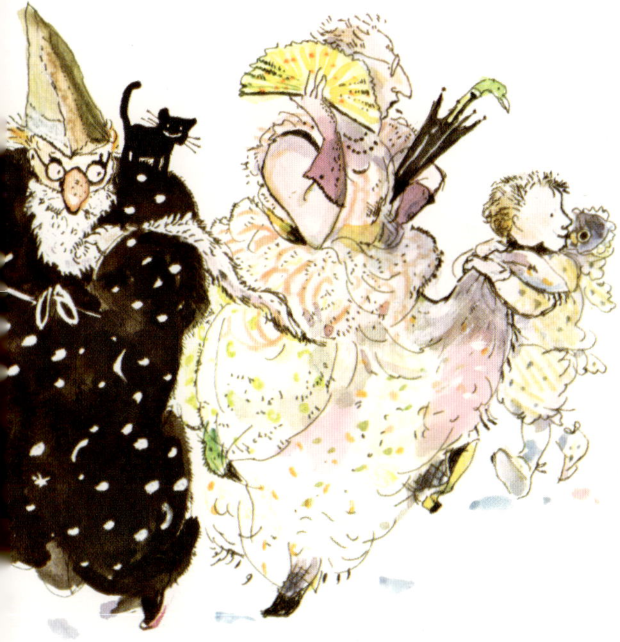

There was Humpty Dumpty.
After him was a birthday cake
and a most beautiful butterfly.

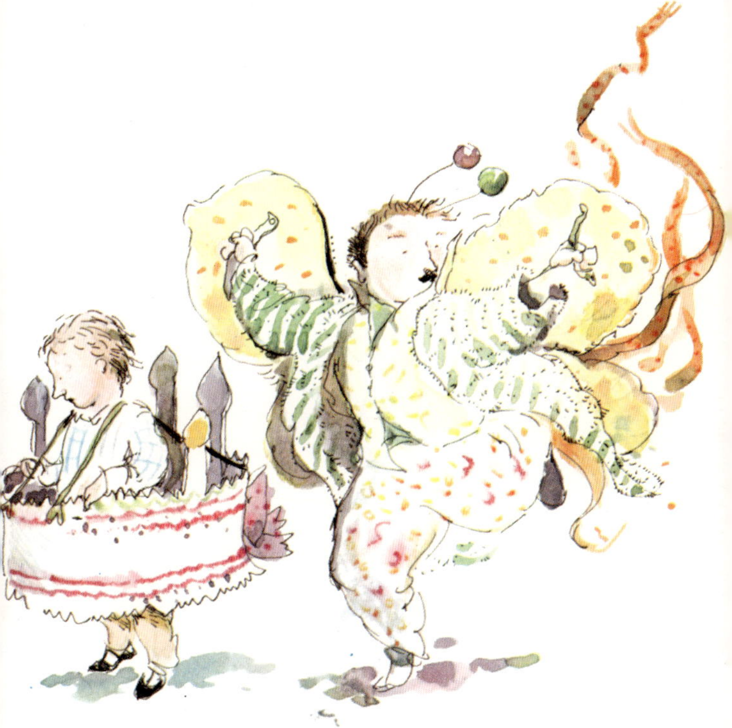

Last of all, there was the pirate
pushed on to the stage
at the very last moment
before he had time to say anything!
He scowled more than ever
and looked very fierce.

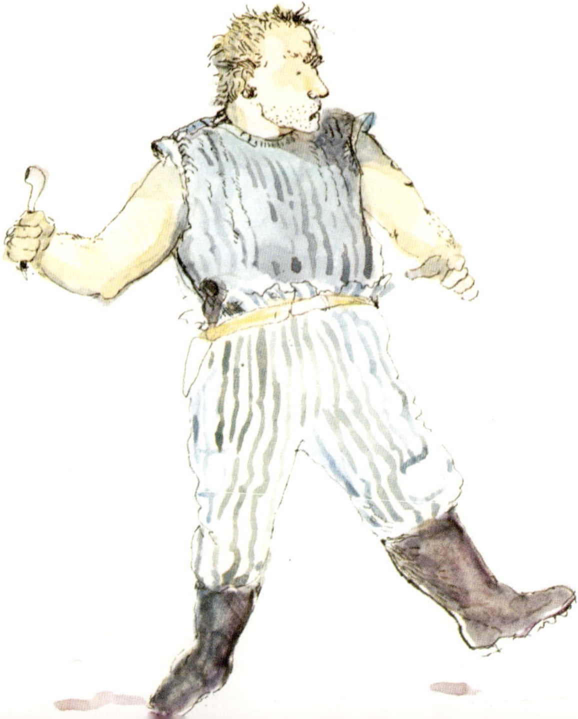

The band stopped playing and the man in the funny tie came back on to the stage holding a piece of paper.

"Here are the winners," he said, "of the grand fancy-dress contest. Third prize goes to the horse, second prize to the birthday cake and first prize ...
to the pirate."

Everyone clapped and cheered
as the pirate went on stage
to collect his prize.

(He was looking rather pleased now.)
The prize was a treasure chest
overflowing with gold coins.

The pirate put the chest
down on the sand and looked at it.
"There's more than enough here
for me to buy a boat.
Here's your share," he said.
He counted out two large piles
of coins.

"And now, my hearties," he said, "I'm off back to sea."
With a large wink, he strode away to the quay.

Tim and Jenny spent a long time
counting their coins.
Jenny looked at hers very carefully.
"Tim," she said, "these aren't real.
They're made of chocolate."

"Well," said Tim, "I don't think
the pirate was real either."
And he pointed out to sea.

There, at the wheel of a fishing boat, was their pirate.
He was puffing his pipe
and watching two fishermen
throwing their net overboard.

Jenny shrugged her shoulders. "Well, we still had a wonderful day out, didn't we?"

MY HOLIDAY LIBRARY

First Edition Copyright © 1983
Reprinted 1984
The Reader's Digest Association
Limited,
25 Berkeley Square, London W1X 6AB

All rights reserved.

® READER'S DIGEST
is a registered trademark of
The Reader's Digest Association, Inc.
of Pleasantville, New York, U.S.A.

Phototypeset by Tradespools Limited,
Frome, Somerset
Printed in Hong Kong